CREATING YOUR SKILLS PORTFOLIO

Show Off Your Skills and Accomplishments

Carrie Straub

A FIFTY-MINUTE™ SERIES BOOK

CREATING YOUR SKILLS PORTFOLIO
Show Off Your Skills and Accomplishments

Carrie Straub

CREDITS
Managing Editor: **Kathleen Barcos**
Editor: **Kay Keppler**
Typesetting: **ExecuStaff**
Cover Design: **Fifth Street Design**
Artwork: **Ralph Mapson**

© 1997 by Crisp Publications, Inc.
Printed in the United States of America by Von Hoffmann Graphics, Inc.

CrispLearning.com

02 03 04   10 9 8 7 6 5 4 3

Library of Congress Catalog Card Number 96-85778
Straub, Carrie
Creating Your Skills Portfolio
ISBN 1-56052-394-8

LEARNING OBJECTIVES FOR:

CREATING YOUR SKILLS PORTFOLIO

The objectives for *Creating Your Skills Portfolio* are listed below. They have been developed to guide you, the reader, to the core issues covered in this book.

Objectives

❑   1) **To explain the functions of a skills portfolio**

❑   2) **To describe the design and production of a skills portfolio**

❑   3) **To present useful strategies for using and presenting a skills portfolio**

Assessing Your Progress

In addition to the learning objectives, Crisp Learning has developed an **assessment** that covers the fundamental information presented in this book. A 25-item, multiple-choice and true-false questionnaire allows the reader to evaluate his or her comprehension of the subject matter. To learn how to obtain a copy of this assessment, please call **1-800-442-7477** and ask to speak with a Customer Service Representative.

Assessments should not be used in any employee selection process.

ABOUT THE AUTHOR

Carrie Straub, MBA, has more than 15 years' experience in the field of human resources. For the past 10 years, she has focused on training and organizational consulting for industry and private industry. She has also been an adjunct instructor at UC Berkeley, South Puget Sound Community College and Clark College.

Carrie has published articles in *Training and Development Journal* and has spoken at Lakewood's Best of America and at national American Society for Training and Development (ASTD) conferences. She is a codeveloper of the model for the State of Washington's award-winning Career Transition Center for State employees.

Acknowledgments

Special thanks and gratitude for the past: Nana and Gammie
Delight in the present: Stan, Blythe, Bonnie, Caleb and Patrick
Hope for the future: Rachel, Caitlin, Charlie V., Lauren and Christian
Who have all contributed so much to my portfolio.

CONTENTS

INTRODUCTION

Creating Your Skills Portfolio is about gaining the critical edge in your job search career or life transition. It offers ways to differentiate yourself from the competition—a key factor in getting what you want.

This book provides opportunities to:

- Analyze what you have to offer an employer based on your productivity—the employment buzzword of the 1990s

- Develop strategies for presenting your skills in a unique format

- Define your area of expertise and what makes work fun for you

- Use a step-by-step process for assessing your experience and building an image

- Gain new skills in personal presentation

- Build your morale and self-image

Any career move (employment change, job search or competition for promotion) is a marketing project, and the product is *you*. A portfolio can make you more visible when you market yourself to employers whether you seek traditional employment, project or temporary work or are starting your own business.

S E C T I O N

1

What Is a Skills Portfolio?

DEFINING "PORTFOLIO"

Photographers, artists, crafts people, graphic designers, interior decorators, models and actors have used portfolios to present their accomplishments for many years. These portfolios often include photographs, drawings, slides, fabric samples, metal work or other objects in addition to written summaries of achievement. Business and government organizations expect a more traditional format, insisting on formal applications, or resumes (sometimes both).

A portfolio is *not a substitute* for a resume. A portfolio is different from a resume in four ways.

#1. Your portfolio may contain 15–30 pages or more. Resumes are expected to be one or two pages at the most.

#2. Your portfolio probably will not stand alone—it will be supported by at least some verbal introduction or explanation.

#3. If you incorporate work samples, photos or original certificates, your portfolio may exist only in the original.

#4. Your resume gets the door open, your portfolio demonstrates the product.

"There is a widespread belief that a great resume will get you a great job," says Marci Mahoney, author of *Strategic Resumes.* "Opportunity will knock and your resume will open the door." She's right, but be sure to bring along your portfolio if you want to capitalize on the opportunities that come your way. Being able to package and market yourself means having the confidence to value your contributions.

WHY YOU SHOULD HAVE A PORTFOLIO

If you have changed jobs in the past 10 years, you know that the days of presenting your resume directly to a prospective employer are over. The information age has made it possible for employers to accumulate candidate pools by capitalizing on job fairs, on-line job posting or outside recruiters, among other strategies. Resumes go to a human resources department and are scanned into a database, sorted by topic and faxed to interested managers. You might get the feeling that your resume would get more notice if you tied it around a brick and tossed it in through a window.

If you are employed by an organization that is large, geographically disbursed or both and you want to grow or change your career path, you can count on competing for opportunities with your peers, outside candidates and possibly even your boss. The hiring manager in product marketing may have no idea of the creative plans your sales support group has implemented. It will be up to you to prove that your experience is transferable.

Current Employment Trends

- Organizations/agencies/divisions merge

- Jobs are transferred away

- Companies shrink/employees are laid off

- Temps are hired to replace permanent workers

- Add your own reason _____

#1. Can you prove that you have the special skills or qualifications that justify retaining you? _____

#2. Will you be able to show that your contributions are critical to the results of the group? _____

#3. If your company is bought out or your unit is transferred to another location, are you prepared to compete for your own job?

_____

> **With a portfolio, you can *show* why you are too valuable to lose.**

Evidence of skills, productivity and experience can make the difference between marking time or landing the position you want. If you are competing with 250 other candidates, you need something that sets you apart.

A portfolio can:

- ☑ Sample your work to show variety and quality

- ☑ Demonstrate work history or chart professional growth

- ☑ Be in print or electronic format

- ☑ Indicate the creative value you added to projects

- ☑ Empower you.

Your portfolio is a marketing tool you can't afford to ignore. It is a powerful strategy that will help give prospective employers ideas about your contributions to their future.

GIVE YOURSELF CREDIT

One question frequently asked about portfolios is, "I was part of a team—what can I take credit for?" The second is, "Was this really important enough to include?"

To build a portfolio and market yourself to a new employer, you must determine and value the contribution you made to your team and use those contributions to define your skills and attributes. The first step is self-awareness: giving yourself the credit you deserve.

After you have defined the elements you contributed to a team or any other effort, identify what would represent those contributions to a prospective employer. That's what goes into your portfolio. Making a decision to hire is expensive and important. Prospective employers will want to see that you can contribute more than you cost.

Your portfolio will be made up of the samples or examples of work that show why you are the best investment a prospective employer can make. The exercises in this workbook will help you review your paid work and volunteer, educational or internship experience. Complete the steps by yourself, work with a peer who knows what you do or ask friends, peers and associates to help you brainstorm the answers. Talk through the exercises and have someone else record the key ideas. At first, include all the examples, ideas and possibilities you think of. Later, you will want to be more selective, depending on the focus of your portfolio.

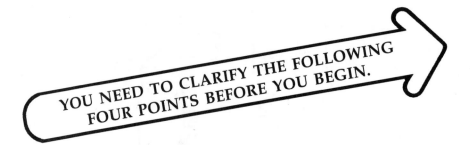

YOU NEED TO CLARIFY THE FOLLOWING FOUR POINTS BEFORE YOU BEGIN.

TYPES OF PORTFOLIOS

Defining parameters for key elements is critical to a successful portfolio. Focusing is frequently ignored or skipped in the rush to ready a portfolio for an interview. Lack of definition shows up in poor organization, inconsistency and frequent reworks of the portfolio. You will need to:

- ► **Clarify Your Message**
- ► **Choose a Medium**
- ► **Set Your Budget**
- ► **Decide on a Static or Dynamic Portfolio**

Clarify Your Message

What do you want your portfolio to show or prove? That you develop the best ad hoc reports in the company? That you simplified tracking forms or flow charts?

Clarifying your message and building your portfolio to get that message across will show in the end product. You will collect dozens—maybe even hundreds—of samples, awards and other "stuff." But are they examples of experiences you want in your future? You may have developed a great management plan from the ground up, but if you never want to do that again in your lifetime, don't show it to an employer as an accomplishment. Now is the time to ask: What's my *Message?*

Message/Mission Statement for My Portfolio

Message: My portfolio shows that I use software programs to create business graphics, forms and documents. It proves that I am fast, accurate, creative and versatile and that I produce more than I cost.

Your Mission Statement:

TYPES OF PORTFOLIOS (continued)

Choose a Medium

What materials will best support your message?

- A newspaper clipping?

- A speaker's badge?

- A diskette with samples of programs you've written?

- Drill core samples that you analyzed?

- Drafts of designs?

Set up a file box or other container with file folders, compartments or other dividers depending on the nature of your tangibles. Dig into the file drawers or archives at work. Look for the photos you took of the conference where you received the Sales Rep of the Year award or the training certificates from your 10 most recent seminars. Gather as much as possible. Later, you can determine which are the best examples of your work. Edit the items you present: Use the clipping and a date line, not the entire page of a newspaper; use only a few pages of the manual you wrote. To help you remember why you wanted to include a specific item, keep the Portfolio Log supplied on page 68.

Note: Use what you can but don't use what you shouldn't. Protect proprietary information by changing names, dates, project titles or other sensitive data. Get *written permission* to use printed materials or copyrighted text.

CASE STUDY: *Consider Consequences*

A state employee had done a project for an agency while employed by a vendor. The project ended and the employee was interviewed by a competing vendor. The portfolio included a report that had been published throughout the industry and was public information. The company reps who saw the report in this context reported to the person's supervisor that they had seen it. Even though public, the employee was required to write a letter explaining why the report was shown.

- Is there anything you will need to get permission to use?

- Would a quote serve as well as the full report?

Set Your Budget

A very credible portfolio can be put together on a shoe string, or you can go for the leather binder with custom-printed dividers. Most portfolios cost about $25 to $50 by the time they are complete; the higher cost includes color copies, a photo, a videotape cassette holder, a leather binder and stationery-quality pages. Be creative.

- Shop the office and art supply stores

- Price-check color copies

- Use the binder you bought and never used

- Check business supply catalogs

- Use desk-top publishing with creativity and consistency.

Decide on a Dynamic or Static Portfolio

Most portfolios are dynamic documents, with things frequently added or deleted. Use a loose-leaf binder so you can rearrange the contents easily. If a diskette or videotape will be part of your portfolio, find out how to lock the contents so they can't be changed, develop an index to speed up the review process and create a colorful label to gain interest.

If this is a one-time-only product (or at least you think so now), you may decide to laminate the portfolio pages or have them bound with a spiral or other binding system. However you assemble your portfolio, don't fold, staple or otherwise mutilate your original—and valuable—documents. Instead, color copy them and keep the originals safely in your scrapbook.

10 WAYS TO USE YOUR PORTFOLIO

Since a portfolio should offer evidence of your experience, capability and skill, its use is not limited to a job search. Brainstorm other times when you could use your portfolio to communicate your skills, talents and accomplishments. Two ideas have been listed to get you started. Check your list with the ideas you'll find as you continue with the exercises in this book.

1. Use it to show what you love to do.

By keeping a spotlight on accomplishments that bring you personal satisfaction, you can put your best foot forward. Talking about the things you value brings a smile to your face and excitement to your voice.

2. Use it in your interview to emphasize your strong points.

By talking about work products and outcomes, you can stay focused on your strengths and skills.

3. _____

4. _____

5. _____

6. _____

7. _____

8. _____

9. _____

10. _____

> *Remember, your portfolio is a personal marketing tool.*
> *Use it to sell yourself.*

SECTION

2

Creating Your Portfolio

FIVE STEPS TO AN EXCELLENT PORTFOLIO

There are five key steps in creating a portfolio that will help you develop a first-rate marketing tool that represents you well.

Step #1:   Gather Artifacts

Review project files, jobs and experience to find the certificates, awards, posters, letters from satisfied customers, performance reviews, presentation evaluations or anything that describes, defines, clarifies or praises. Store these in a record storage container for easy reference.

Step #2:   Visualize Your Portfolio

Think about the sequence, graphics and layout of your portfolio. What message do you want to convey? Advance thinking will increase the visual impact. Planning will help build consistency, message and communication.

Step #3:   Organize Your Information

Once you have all your information collected, evaluate each piece. Edit the material to ensure that each piece is relevant to the message you want to get across—the content, consistency and communication impact of your portfolio. Ask for feedback and be sure to listen!

Step #4:   Assemble the Contents

How you assemble your portfolio is critical to its success. Your design and lay-out must look professional and clearly articulate your talents and achievements. It should identify you, enhance your credibility and project your capabilities.

Step #5:   Practice Your Presentation

Develop your presentation. Know what you will say about each page and practice introducing the items. Practice delivering your information using a tape recorder or a live audience.

STEP #1: GATHER ARTIFACTS

List some things that you might include in your portfolio. Try to develop a list of at least 10 possibilities. As you progress through the exercises in this book, you will find that the list will grow and you will have the happy challenge of selecting the most impressive.

Samples/Examples

1. _____

2. _____

3. _____

4. _____

5. _____

6. _____

7. _____

8. _____

9. _____

10. _____

EXERCISE: *Asking Key Questions*

After you have finished your list, answer the following questions to help you bring the information into better focus.

	Yes	No
1. Are you considering several career paths?	☐	☐
2. Do you need more than one portfolio?	☐	☐
3. Is your experience extremely varied (for example, finish carpentry, bookkeeping and organizing action-oriented training programs)?	☐	☐
4. Have you changed careers in the past?	☐	☐
5. Has your career taken a different direction through a promotion or transfer?	☐	☐
6. Will your experience look confusing or scattered?	☐	☐
7. Does your list show skills, capabilities or experience that you do not want to use in future jobs?	☐	☐
8. Will these get you a job just like the one you are trying to leave?	☐	☐

CONDUCT A MARKET ANALYSIS OF YOU AS A PRODUCT

Interviewers often ask, "Why should I hire you?" In this exercise, you can develop the answer to that question. After you complete your market analysis, proceed to the "Value Added" review.

What do I have to offer an employer?

For this exercise, work with a partner, if possible. Tell your partner about your abilities and achievements, and what difference those have made in your work. Consider what you liked about your jobs and why. Use the interview questions below to stimulate your thinking. Talk through your answers and have your partner jot down notes in the space provided. Think of your answers—your description of your skills and attributes—as a product that you can sell to an employer.

1. What are three words that describe the strengths you bring to any job?

_____

_____

_____

2. How do those strengths contribute to your career?

_____

_____

_____

3. What have you collected (or could you collect) that would demonstrate these strengths?

_____

_____

_____

4. What are the tasks or duties you like best?

_____

_____

_____

5. What skills, knowledge or achievements you are most proud of?

_____

_____

_____

6. What results or accomplishments would you like to demonstrate or prove?

_____

_____

_____

7. What do your supervisors and coworkers think you do well?

_____

_____

_____

8. List an example of the last time you did this.

_____

_____

_____

CONDUCT A MARKET ANALYSIS OF YOU AS A PRODUCT (continued)

9. List the ways you have been praised about your work.

_____

_____

_____

10. What tangibles (projects, awards, certifications, products) have been mentioned in your performance appraisals?

_____

_____

_____

ACTION ITEM: Collect copies of written performance appraisals, e-mails and company announcements for your artifact file.

VALUE-ADDED ACHIEVEMENTS AND ACCOMPLISHMENTS

Working above and beyond expectations—that's what we mean by value-added effort. In today's competitive employment environment, you may compete with hundreds of other applicants for a job, promotion or project. Take this opportunity to identify the extra effort, the added contributions and improvements you've made. Did you:

- ▶ Eliminate a three-year backlog of work in six months by allocating workflow more effectively?

- ▶ Add a quality-control step without increasing the amount of time the activity took?

- ▶ Reorganize delivery routes and truck loads so they were more efficient?

- ▶ Improve customer satisfaction while eliminating mistakes in delivery?

- ▶ Serve as a department representative on a safety team that reduced accidents with the new procedures?

Include value-added accomplishments from your work life, your volunteer life and your personal life. Complete the next exercise by including as much as possible. If you doubt the legitimacy of the value you added, use a "flip-side technique": Think about how costs would have risen, problems that would have continued or customers would have gone elsewhere if things had gone on the way they were.

The value-added accomplishments are frequently the starting point for a career change because we find we have made an exceptional contribution in a new situation. Showcase these to provide a basis for transferable skills when you haven't had the specific title. For example, perhaps you learned a presentation software and your title was "word processor," yet you were the person who did all department transparencies for executive briefings.

EXERCISE: Get Specific

Have you volunteered for a task force or employee committee or performed community service? What contribution did the group make? Did you redo all the overheads for routine orientation and learn a new software to do it? Do you have the "before" and "after"?

> Identify the value you added to your group and the achievements for which you've been praised. Using the worksheet, note at least three areas of responsibility, your accomplishments in those areas and the project results.

Beginning with your present job, list what you have learned or accomplished.

Areas of Responsibility	Accomplishment	Output/Work Product
Project activity tracking	Set up action-step tracking document on the LAN, which allowed team members to enter data as steps were completed	Screen print of document, weekly report to manager, written report to client

Reviewing past jobs or projects, list what you learned or accomplished. Immediacy is important: focus on the past 10 years unless it was a Presidential Award or Nobel Prize or has direct bearing on the career you plan to pursue.

Areas of Responsibility	Accomplishment	Output/Work Product

ACTION ITEM: Collect "before" and "after" samples, committee reports, photos and written descriptions of task force efforts. Develop process maps to show the steps eliminated, number of clients who received service or proposals that were developed.

EXERCISE: *Defining Your Achievements*

Using the list you developed earlier, brainstorm how you could represent your work.

What You Did	Samples That Would Represent This	Required Items
Created new tracking database for Xanadu Excursion	Printout of raw data and pie chart of monthly results	Printout without user ID and sample pie chart

Many accomplishments come from volunteer or other life experience. What skills have you gained that are related to the new job or career you want to pursue? List affiliations or memberships that could be included in your portfolio. Think about the talents or interest needed to fit in here.

Affiliation/ Membership	Talent Skill	Samples That Would Demonstrate These

COLLECTING SAMPLES

Based on the list you created on page 14, restate five specific topics or samples of work items you want to include in your portfolio.

List elements of these items that would raise your interest if you were an audience consisting of:

Members of a hiring panel from a state agency

_____

_____

_____

The human resources recruiter from a company opening a new facility in the area

_____

_____

_____

The manager of a work team in a small, family-owned business

_____

_____

_____

What else could you include from your past experience that would be of interest to the audiences mentioned?

_____

_____

_____

EXPLORING POSSIBILITIES

Ask yourself (and others) what message you get from each item you include in your portfolio. What's the point of including it? Does it tell a skill story? Does it mention an accomplishment or experience applicable to the job you are seeking?

Why include a photo of yourself in an outdated uniform? To make the point that you've been there a long time? Length of time in a position is not necessarily a virtue. What you produced or accomplished is relevant.

You also need not include all reports, photos and prizes. A few representative pages of a report will get the idea across. Be selective. Your audience's time is limited.

What's Too Old to Be Included?

Recent accomplishments and examples are best. If you are using the thematic sequence, focus on gathering more recent examples (the last three to seven years). If you are using a chronological sequence, you will want to include something from all of your work periods; again, include fewer examples from previous jobs than present. However, if you were awarded a Presidential Citation for Community Service 15 years ago, include it— perhaps by putting it in a special section.

The exception to the rule of immediacy is when you want to return to a career you left behind or capitalize on experience that isn't present in your job today. If that's the case, include examples from the past as needed to establish credibility.

One way to include items that are from the beginning of your career history: Include a section titled "Other Relevant Accomplishments." Do not specify dates for the items in this section. In this way you can include your experience to round out your capabilities without seeming out of date.

PLAY "PORTFOLIO BINGO"

Portfolio Bingo

Here are examples of work products that could be in your portfolio. Your Bingo card is a winner when you have added three items to at least five of the areas. You may add other work products in addition to those shown below.

B	I	N	G	O
Brochures	Information Reports	Newsletters	Graphs	Operations Examples
Books	Improvements	News Releases	Gratitude (thank you letters, etc.)	Outlines
Background Research	Ideas	**FREE**	Graphics	*_____
*_____	Innovations and Inventions	Negotiations	Gifts	Official Transcripts
Biographies	Imple-mentations	New Systems (filing, work flow, data distribution)	Good Evaluations	Organi-zational Examples

*Insert your own ideas

ACTION ITEM: Now that you've listed the many possibilities, take time to find them, start a file and get copies.

EXPLORING POSSIBILITIES (continued)

Selecting References

The best references are from those with whom you've worked recently or those who have a high degree of name recognition and credibility. A four-year-old letter of reference from a Supreme Court justice beats out a luke-warm recommendation from a current supervisor every time. If you are ever asked to write your own letter of reference, remember to be specific about your accomplishments and contribution to the goals of the organization.

If you know your references will be contacted, call them to let them know. Tell them what you have done recently and what they might be asked about. (Nothing will damage your credibility as much as the reference who says, "I haven't kept track of Terry for the last few years.")

Personal and Professional Experience

If you have pursued both a vocation and an avocation (perhaps served on the city board of supervisors or held a leadership post in volunteer search and rescue operations) and want to show the range of your paid and unpaid experience to qualify for a career change, this format may fit the best. Arrange your experience on a topical basis. Using labels such as leadership, personal accomplishments, community involvement or relevant education will help your audience remember your skills and capabilities.

Electronic Media

Modern communication lets us send resumes and applications by fax and e-mail, use our computers to search for job postings from Aberdeen to Zillah or have our own home page on the Internet so employers can come to us. Your resume and portfolio should contain your e-mail address and fax number, if you have them. Make diskettes of your portfolio. You may be asked for copies of documents, or even to loan your entire portfolio. Offering a diskette is a diplomatic way of refusing to part with your hard copy.

STRATEGY ALERT

► If you want to put some of your work examples on a diskette, use a common software such as Excel™ or Word™, or some other industry-standard program. Lock the files so they can't be changed or lifted. Offer this diskette whether or not you are asked to leave a sample.

► Respond to on-line job announcements or ads with an edited version of your portfolio. Scanning makes it possible to include one-of-a-kind items as attachments to e-mail messages.

► Show off your technology skills by developing a multimedia package that comes on diskette. For good examples, get on the Internet and visit Joe Mack's Job Seek Module on the World Wide Web or check out Intel's recruiting announcements.

► Although your portfolio may be in a format that isn't accessible by your prospective employer, formats are fairly easy to translate. When you develop your electronic portfolio, invest a few dollars to have it translated into several of the most common platforms.

► Using a desktop presentation software such as PowerPoint™ or Persuasion™ is fun but may not be practical, since it's important to be spontaneous when presenting your portfolio in person. However, these software products can be used effectively to develop a presentation that you leave behind, one that walks through your experience step by step. Graphics, charts, color and imports from other software packages can make these slide shows sizzle.

STEP #2: VISUALIZE YOUR PORTFOLIO

Evolving a thought, idea or image into a finished page in your portfolio requires visualization. While artists may be able to complete this process inside their creative imagination, most of us require a pencil and paper at the very least. It's a common error for people to think that they can go to the finished product without any of the intermediate steps.

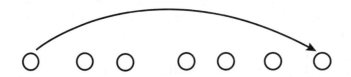

The common error is to go to the finished product in one jump.

Four good reasons to visualize your portfolio before you assemble it include:

#1. You'll have a more satisfactory product at the end of the project

#2. You'll spend less time on it. You won't have to redo it as often

#3. You'll reduce the possibilities of defacing or ruining the only copy of some sample

#4. You'll spend less money if you plan before you begin production. You won't waste as much paper or purchase items you ultimately decide not to use

THE VISUALIZATION PROCESS

Stage 1: Do Your Homework

Complete the worksheets and collect the artifacts, samples and examples. Analyze your audience. Use projection—put yourself into someone else's shoes—to decide what will best reveal your experiences and capabilities to the audience you want to reach.

Stage 2: Make Thumbnail Sketches

Sketch out thumbnails of the most important items to be included. Thumbnails are small, quick, idea sketches. Post-it notes are excellent for this purpose because they make the next step much easier. You can resolve many questions and eliminate many problems in the thumbnail stage.

Thumbnail Sketches

Be sure that the thumbnails you develop show the basic layout of the page. This will help as you plan the sequence in the storyboard.

Remember: The portfolio should be able to show samples to an audience of one or more persons. Having to turn the book to a different position will affect how easy it is to display the information. Your thumbnails will also be useful when you decide what, where and how any labels or other signals need to be applied.

THE VISUALIZATION PROCESS (continued)

Try it out! Develop some thumbnails of your examples in the spaces below.

Stage 3: Develop a Storyboard

A storyboard is a group of sketches that tell your story in sequence—including dividers, examples and written explanations. Index cards, Post-it notes and copies of the documents or samples that have been reduced to thumbnail size are helpful, but a storyboard can be developed simply by drawing squares on a blank sheet of paper and filling them in.

A storyboard is a valuable planning tool because it forces you to reassess your content and review the logic of your display sequence. You can't show off all your skills and experience equally in each situation, but your portfolio needs to have balance and coherence in all the segments.

Your portfolio is a tool to create a unique image of your experience that makes it easy to remember. Rather than drowning your audience with an example of everything you've done, use the best examples to make your point.

People tend to see visual images as common patterns, in the left-to-right, top-to-bottom sequence. Lines suggest movement, so adding a horizontal arrow to direct your viewer from a picture to the comments you have written will help focus attention where you want it.

A storyboard is a road map of your portfolio. Use it to plan your trip.

NOW IT'S YOUR TURN TO GET CREATIVE!

THE VISUALIZATION PROCESS (continued)

Storyboard Practice

Try your hand at organizing the material you want to include in your portfolio. Use quick sketches, a few words or Post-its for now.

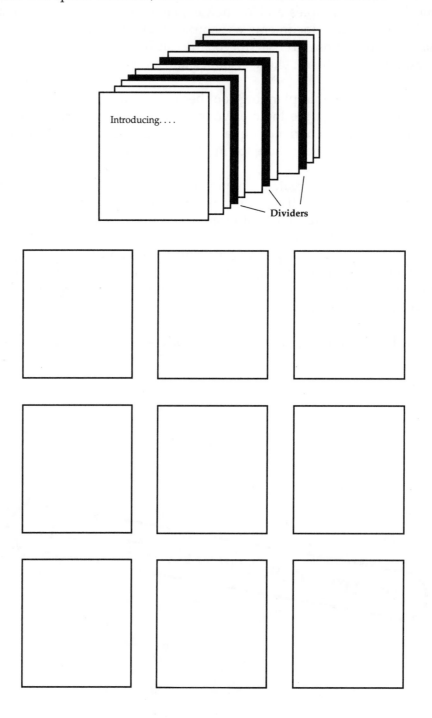

STEP #3: ORGANIZE YOUR INFORMATION

Plan, plan, plan! Getting there is easy if you know where you're going. However, you still must make more decisions if you are to have a finished product that you will be proud to display to a potential employer.

Worksheet

Do a Structure Analysis

What sequence will accomplish my mission best?

_____

_____

What is my audience accustomed to "seeing"? What level of knowledge can I expect them to have?

_____

_____

Is it most logical to show all of my data flow design projects together, then give examples of programs I've written? Or is it better to show what I did as a Research Analyst 1, then as Associate 3?

_____

_____

_____

_____

The Bottom Line
Will a thematic or a chronological sequence tell a better tale?

STEP #3 (continued)

Decide on a Focused or General Approach

Will there be only one model of my portfolio? Should my portfolio have my complete life in it, just in case?

_____

_____

Do I want them to know that I am qualified as a real estate appraiser as well as a project manager? Will that information only distract from my real message?

_____

_____

$M + A + M = I^2$

$M + A + M = I^2$ (Message + Audience + Medium = Impact/Importance)

Each item you include, each border you add, each time you tape yourself during a sales training session demonstrates the composite you. These elements of your portfolio determine its impact on the audience that will examine it.

The format of your portfolio is as critical to its message as the content. Define and plan ahead, then get lots of feedback. Play around with the elements to ensure that you deliver the right message to the intended audience.

If you find it difficult to edit because everything seems important, collect brochures about your favorite topic. Examine them for image and evaluate how they deliver their message. Notice how magazines get their theme across.

Sequential/Chronological Order

The sequential or chronological format is often the preferred format for resumes because it is organized around your employment history. In your portfolio, you should represent your career accomplishments in the sequence in which they occurred if:

☐ Your career has followed a linear, progressive path

☐ Your track record shows you clearly qualified for a specific level of position

☐ You want to show that your experience has qualified you for succeeding with specific job challenges.

You may divide sections by years or time period, job title or promotion, or company or organization.

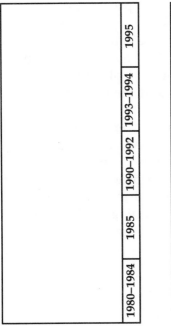
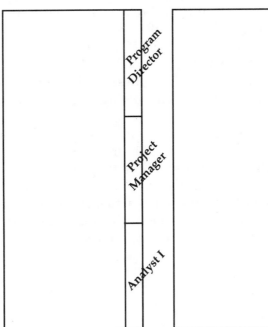

STEP #3 (continued)

Thematic/Functional Format

Your experience and capabilities are the basic organizing principles of this format. Include both paid and unpaid experience, skills and accomplishments. Consider representing your career accomplishments in this sequence if:

- [ ] You are changing careers and want to show a combination of experiences that qualify you

- [ ] You want to transfer experience from one industry to another

- [ ] You have worked on special projects or have accomplishments that aren't well represented by the title you've held or years of experience you've gained

- [ ] You want to accentuate skills and experience in a variety of industries.

The thematic categories that name the functions represented in your portfolio are endless. You can use skill-related titles such as word processing, record keeping or programming. Titles that show your professional experiences (sales, creative advertising and PR, management administration) are useful in communicating functional areas of your experience. You may want to consider words that describe activities, such as analyzing and planning, writing/research, liaison and problem solving or negotiation and mediation.

Use category descriptions that give you a lead-in for answering the interview question, "What is your greatest strength?" You reply, "My planning ability is a strength I've been praised for frequently. For example, I was assigned to a project that was behind schedule. Let me show you a project task plan and time line I built to compare the actual from the target. (Bring out your portfolio and turn to the page in the analyzing and planning section.) This allowed us to plan ways to correct deficiencies quickly. Notice how. . . ."

Layout and Design

Graphic design is an art in itself. Professional designers spend years learning the fundamental techniques of visual communication. You may never become a graphic designer, but learning a few basic rules will make your portfolio more readable and interesting. Two issues need to be considered when designing the layout of the pages and graphics of your portfolio.

#1. Self-expression—your personal creativity—which must be balanced by the second

#2. The need to satisfy an audience in a logical manner within economic limits.

Applying graphic design to your portfolio is a critical requirement, not a cosmetic afterthought. Good design enhances communication and creates an image of you. Effective design uses:

- Typography

- Placement of elements (work samples, letters, certificates)

- Symbols (labels, header/footers)

- Illustration

- Color and white space.

These all combine to achieve a visually interesting product.

CONSIDER THE AUDIENCE

We are inundated every day with ads, posters, billboards—every kind of print campaign, much of which has been designed to inform and persuade and which has had a development budget of thousands or hundreds of thousands of dollars.

This means that you are competing for attention with a visually sophisticated audience.

However, you are probably showing your portfolio to an audience of your peers—people who have about the same work experience as you and share the same jargon and technical expertise. Let's examine a few basics to ensure appropriate layout for that audience.

THREE LAYOUT BASICS

1. *Reading Flow.* In western cultures, we read left to right, top to bottom. You will need to take this eye flow into account when placing elements such as labels, photos, illustrations or work samples on a page.

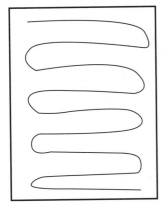
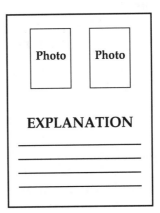

2. *Eye Scan.* The human eye favors the lower left hand area of any field rather than the center of the field. The eye tends to rest there and return there. Place important points at the bottom left of the page. That way, the people who review the page will see what you choose to show more often if your portfolio is left open in front of them.

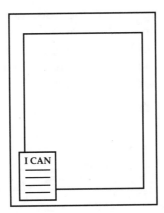

3. *Vision.* People in your audience may have faulty eyesight. Color blindness may impair communication. Therefore, use 9-point type or larger and high-contrast colors or reverse type (white letters on black backgrounds) to sharpen contrast and improve legibility.

This is 8 point type

This is reverse 8 point type

THREE LAYOUT BASICS (continued)

Use visual identity to enhance your message. Visual identity is the visible essence of any entity—person, division, company or government agency. The choice of visual identity reflects the style and self-image of the body it represents.

EXERCISE: *Visual Identity*

What are some of the most recognizable visual identities in the world?

- Coke's logo

- IBM's logo

- Disney's Mickey Mouse ears

Others: _____

_____

_____

Symbols, logos and pictographs help the audience build a visual frame of reference. Arrows or dots direct attention to items or ideas. By creating labels, tabs and headers or footers with consistent, logical use throughout your portfolio, you can lay out a visual frame of reference that will help anyone who reviews your portfolio understand your experience.

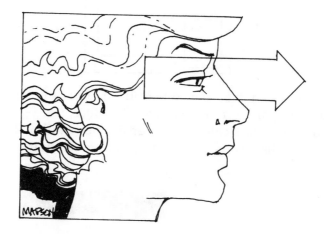

10 TIPS FOR BETTER VISUAL ORGANIZATION

We are visually oriented: Retention increases by more than 50% when information presented verbally is supported with visuals. Written information should be brief and supported with graphs, cartoons, schematics, block diagrams and scale or line drawings.

1. Using a border or frame around the page or picture gives it a finished look.

2. Color increases interest and retention.

3. Use color to accentuate, not decorate.

4. We assign strong cultural significance to color. Do some research about this and select your theme accordingly.

5. In Western cultures, we read from left to right, top to bottom. When eyes are at rest, they focus on the bottom left quadrant of the page. This is the hotspot for important messages.

6. Business readers are in a hurry. They scan, so use lots of white space and headlines for interest.

7. Using more than two type faces per page makes it difficult to concentrate on the message.

8. Use bold or italic, cap and lower case type and borders or screens for emphasis. Use them sparingly.

9. Make the complex simple.

10. People prefer to view things in patterns. Create a theme and stick to it.

STEP #4: ASSEMBLE THE CONTENTS

Shop your stationery, office supply and art supply stores for materials. The generic list of ingredients will give you some ideas. Choose your materials based on the image you want to achieve.

Recipe for Success

INGREDIENTS

1	3-ring binder (approximately 1 inch)*
20 to 30	3-hole drilled mylar sheet protectors
1 pkg.	4 or 5 cut divider tabs (optional)
4 or 5	colors of paper—enough sheets to use for backing and color strips
4 or 5	colors of tape (optional)
1	labeling machine or laser printer w/label software
1	3-hole drilled plastic holder for diskettes (optional)
1 or 2	diskettes
1 pkg.	laser-transfer foil to make customer borders or covers (optional)
1 pkg.	colored dots or other highlighters (optional)
3 or 4	copies of examples to keep behind the originals
	sharp scissors
	transparent tape
	Post-it tape (white removable tape that has the sticky qualities of Post-it notes)
	glue
	ruler

*Use binders covered in cloth, leather, vinyl or those that allow a cover sheet to be slipped into a pocket. Insta-Cover Display Books have the mylar sheet protectors permanently bound and come in a variety of sizes, including those with six, 12 and 20 pockets. The standard size 8-1/2" × 11" binder is most common. Smaller sizes may not display materials well. Larger sizes may be awkward to carry.

Directions for Easy Assembly

#1. Plan the visual image. Prepare thumbnails of your documents and experiment with layout. Develop a storyboard—a pencil draft that will help you determine the logic of sequence for the pages, dividers and "story." See pages 29–32 for more on storyboards and thumbnails.

#2. Select a 3-ring binder that has the image you want. Insert the divider tabs (use the color-coded type that has a contents sheet that will go through your laser printer) or install your custom-made dividers.

#3. If you are using color-coded tabs, organize sections according to the thematic or chronological sequence, determine appropriate title for each section and print table of contents. If you are custom designing your dividers, develop graphics and titles, and print them. Use the laser-transfer foil to highlight your name on the cover, border clippings or as a stripe to add interest to pages.

> **Idea!**
>
> If you use articles from newsletters or newspapers, clip them out, with a date line. Using colored paper, print a border a little larger than the clipping, mount clipping with glue and highlight the key ideas.

#4. Assemble your examples in sheet protectors, color code, highlight and label them.

#5. Develop a lead-in statement or brief explanation of each item, which includes an explanation of the accomplishment, why it's an important example of your work and how the experience would contribute to the situation you are seeking.

STEP #4 (continued)

How Much Is Too Much?

As a rule of thumb, your portfolio should be no larger than 20–30 pages. The following are guidelines based on what experience shows will gain the interviewer's interest and demonstrate the candidate's strengths without intimidating or irritating the interviewer. However, this question of length is one to be answered by your own judgment and experience.

Chronological	Thematic
Fewer than 20 pages, including	Up to 30 pages, including
Resume Reference list	Resume Reference list
Most recent experience 8–10 pages	Function A 4–6 pages
Previous job or career 3–5 pages	Function B 4–6 pages
Previous 2–3 pages Very Important	Function C 4–6 pages
Letters of Reference, Awards, Citations	Awards, Letters of Commendation

10 TIPS FOR A BETTER PORTFOLIO

There are a few simple steps you can take to ensure that your portfolio is both professional-looking and dynamic.

TIP #1   Remember That Less Is More

Your audience usually gets just a brief glance at your portfolio, so whatever you include must be clear and memorable. Use one or two, instead of six or seven, photos taken at the conference you coordinated, with a brief description of its size, budget and duration.

Photo of you and your trusty computer . . .

Let me show you what my flying fingers can do for you . . .

Experiment with type size, but generally use a rather large size.

10 TIPS FOR A BETTER PORTFOLIO (continued)

TIP #2 | Use the Salami Method

Producing a portfolio is a time-consuming project, so slice it up. Setting aside small blocks of time for the steps is easier than trying to do it all at once.

Example

Activity Slice	Time Allotted	Target Completion Date
Complete the exercises in this workbook	1 hour	1 week from today
Set up a file or storage box	20 minutes	2 days from today
Assemble photos, reports, examples	30 minutes per day	Daily for 3 weeks
Determine sequence: thematic or chronological		
Develop pencil draft of page layout		
Gather materials (binder, laminating)		

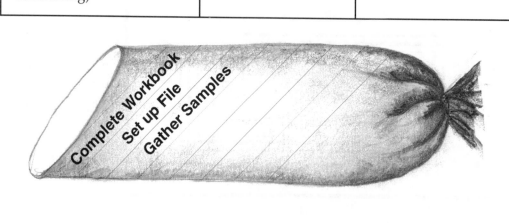

TIP #3 | Prioritize Your Examples

Weed out examples until you have 20–30 pages, including the title pages and dividers. You might want to include more examples, but evaluate each carefully to determine what it adds to your portfolio.

SOFTWARE AND GRAPHIC SKILLS

Software used in this portfolio:
WordPerfect 6.0
MS Word 6
Excel 5

Sample divider page

10 TIPS FOR A BETTER PORTFOLIO
(continued)

| TIP #4 | **Beta Test** |

Show your portfolio to friends, colleagues and family. Practice your commercial announcements on them. Write down their questions. Assess your portfolio against their comments and decide what else needs to be included and what needs to be taken out.

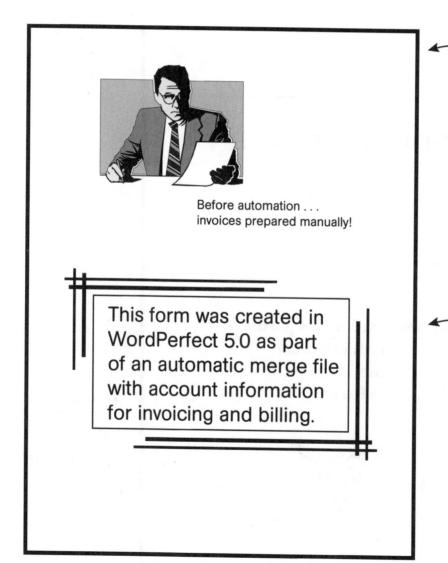

Before automation . . .
invoices prepared manually!

This form was created in WordPerfect 5.0 as part of an automatic merge file with account information for invoicing and billing.

Use clip art sparingly and keep it professional.

Include explanations about your sample that are brief and easy to comprehend.

TIP #5 | Respect Confidential and Proprietary Information

Use only work that is available to the public. Describe the project results, write sample reports, include a promotional marketing brochure, use the title slide from a financial report presentation, but NEVER reveal secrets that are not yours.

If you are planning to leave a copy of something that although not confidential, is not for general distribution, label it "For Evaluation Only—Not to Be Copied or Disclosed."

STATISTICAL GRAPHS

- These samples were taken from Crisis Clinic telephone statistics.

- I originally produced them using Revelation database software.

- Excel and MS Word were used for the charts.

Protect your examples. Rather than identifying the Crisis Clinic as the source, say "These samples were taken from Telephone Statistics" and tell how they were produced and formatted.

10 TIPS FOR A BETTER PORTFOLIO
(continued)

TIP #6 Treat Coworkers with Respect

Do not show your coworkers in a bad light. Rather than including a memo from someone else with errors you corrected, include a report you wrote. Making your colleagues look bad makes you look bad, too.

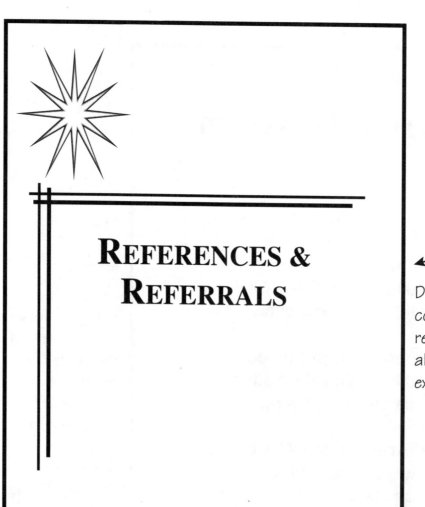

REFERENCES & REFERRALS

Don't forget to contact your references and alert them to expect a call.

TIP #7 | Consider Having More Than One Portfolio

If you had several careers or have a hobby that you'd like to pursue as a vocation, consider developing more than one portfolio. You could develop a combination portfolio that presents your paid experience with your desired career, but developing two separate portfolios could be easier to manage and discuss.

> The final product of a complex process—let there be an advance sheet!!

Experiment with using a different design and a different type size and font on your second portfolio.

10 TIPS FOR A BETTER PORTFOLIO
(continued)

TIP #8 | Color Code, Label and Simplify

You will want to be able to find your example quickly. Make it easy to find what you want to show. If you are using mylar sheet protectors, color code them by running a narrow colored band down the side of the page (say green for project reports, blue for letters of reference). When labeling flyers, photos, and other material, use a label on the outside of the mylar holder—don't mar your original by sticking things directly on it. Number the pages.

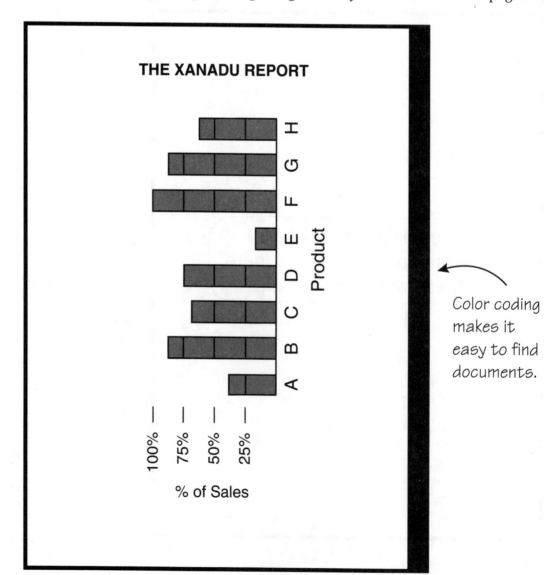

Color coding makes it easy to find documents.

TIP #9 Use a Consistent Format

The contents of your portfolio should grow and change as your career does. New work products, new ideas about what to include or new opportunities for growth will require updates. Use consistent graphics and layout throughout. Tie diverse documents together by using consistent label format and bordering background pages.

DOCUMENT PREPARATION

Notice how the font, type size, border style and star matches what was used in Tip #6.

10 TIPS FOR A BETTER PORTFOLIO (continued)

TIP #10 Use a Skill Summary

This summary can be placed at the beginning or the end of the portfolio. Leave your portfolio open to this page each time you finish presenting an example so that if the interviewer looks at your portfolio, he or she will get your skill summary every time.

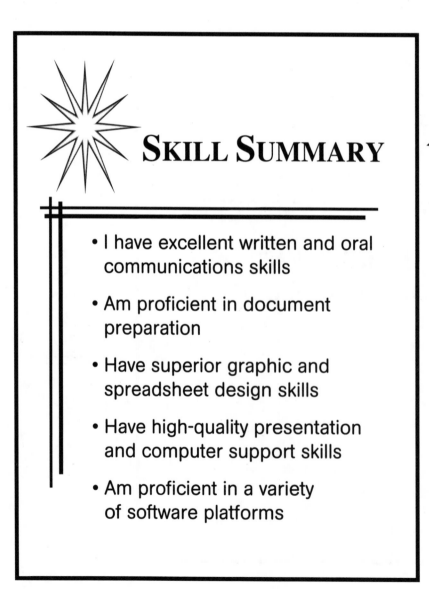

SKILL SUMMARY

- I have excellent written and oral communications skills

- Am proficient in document preparation

- Have superior graphic and spreadsheet design skills

- Have high-quality presentation and computer support skills

- Am proficient in a variety of software platforms

Say what the page is about.

REFERENCES FOR THE GRAPHICALLY IMPAIRED

If you need to include photos or samples in your portfolio, take special care to present them in the most effective way.

Presenting Photos

Select one or two photos that show energy or action and have good color contrast and are in focus. Mount them on the page with a brief explanation of their meaning. Adding a border around the photo will give a finished look to the page. Use the same technique when you include a newspaper clipping or an item from the company newsletter. Use desktop publishing software to lay out the page and border, then tape or laminate the photos in place. You can also use the graphics tape available in art stores.

If you have several photos that should be presented together, arrange them on the left page and include an explanation, copy of the conference budget or analysis of the conference evaluations on the right page. This setup allows easy explanations as you point to the information you want noticed.

REFERENCES FOR THE GRAPHICALLY IMPAIRED (continued)

Masking and Retouching

If you have a document, photo or other example that is in poor condition, you may want to "mask" or retouch it. Let's say that the edges of your certificate are dog-eared, the first page of the report has coffee stains or someone has taken notes in the margin of an article in which your achievement was featured.

You can hide the borders (or "mask" them out) by using another sheet of paper and cutting a window in it that leaves room to show only what you want to show from the original document. If the mask is decorative or otherwise suitable, you can display it in your portfolio. Otherwise, copy the certificate onto a certificate paper, which is available from office supply stores.

Post-it tape also does an amazing job of cleaning up the report where someone took notes or blocking out names and numbers to protect confidentiality. Apply the tape to cover mistakes and deletions.

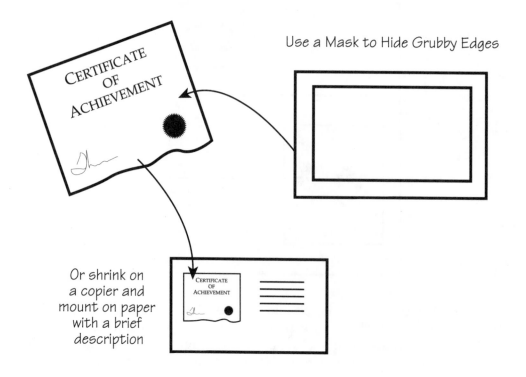

Use a Mask to Hide Grubby Edges

Or shrink on a copier and mount on paper with a brief description

Managing 3-D Samples

Perhaps you're an archeologist, and your portfolio should contain artifacts. Or you're a geologist, inventor, antiques restorer or costume designer. It would be difficult to include the objects you found, classified, built or created—but you can include representations of your work. Try laying them out on a copier, putting a sheet of poly-foam over them and making a copy.

Make use of new technology. Can the samples be scanned? Could you use computer modeling to reconstruct them? Digital cameras can be of great help. Many copy centers have digital cameras that take photos of objects by digitizing the image and storing it on a diskette. The image then can be manipulated in desktop publishing and printed directly on your laser printer.

Using Technology

Computer diskettes

Other new technologies are getting cheaper and easier to use. Consider whether any of them could improve your portfolio. Work samples on diskette are excellent "leave-behinds" for your prospective employer to evaluate your work. They can also be mailed with a cover letter as stand-alone marketing tactics when you are trying to create interest in your skills.

Video tapes

A video of you leading a class, directing the orchestra, planting a shrub, assembling your computer or taking the dents out of a fender will both impress a prospective employer with your capability and show that you know how to market yourself.

Home video equipment can produce an adequate tape. Editing and adding titles or music can be done for around $100, depending on length and complexity. Your phone book yellow pages will list editing studios that can polish your product. (Public access television usually offers training in production and camera technique very cheaply.) Post-production cost for the tape you record is small. VHS half-inch format is the industry standard for playback in the United States, so don't use 8mm or other formats unless you are sending your tape to another country. In that case, find out what VCR format is most used in that area.

REFERENCES FOR THE GRAPHICALLY IMPAIRED (continued)

CD-ROM

This new technology accommodates large text files with video and audio. You could display newsletters you designed or tell the story of the project from start to finish. Slides, still photos, and video clips are relatively inexpensive to transfer. Computer-generated production is becoming easier and cheaper with the read/write technology now available. Most production copy centers can produce a CD-ROM for you. Costs to "print" vary wildly, so shop around.

Multimedia Checklist

Follow simple steps in this checklist to make those diskettes, tapes and other media much more effective.

☐ Use laser-printed labels: name the file and include your name, address and phone number on the label.

☐ Be brief. Show the name of the file, the software that will be needed to open and view it and the date it was created. Put this information on the label, if it fits. Otherwise include the information in your cover letter.

☐ Use a common name for the position you are seeking: process flow analyst, public information officer, senior secretary, program manager.

☐ Include a mailer with envelope and postage if you want the media returned; assume it won't be sent back, though. If you get it back, you'll be pleasantly surprised.

☐ Put a copyright notation on the label if the material is your original creation and you own the copyrights. If you do not wish the contents used without your permission but you don't want a copyright notation, say: "For evaluation purposes only. Not to be used or disclosed without permission."

☐ Check office supply stores for pocket holders that hold the tape or diskette in your portfolio. Make a second copy of the tape so it can be left for review.

Clip Art

Cartoons, arrows, lines and other artwork should be used to accentuate, not decorate. If someone describes the image as "cute," take it out. (Unless you design children's clothing or toys, cute is *not* a word you want connected with your career achievements.) However, a consistent logo, border around photos or drawings or unique type style on the cover page can contribute to a professional-looking portfolio.

Use clip art sparingly.

STEP #5: PRACTICE YOUR PRESENTATION

Your portfolio probably will not be a stand-alone document. You also need to develop and practice what you want to say about the examples you've included.

Take a few minutes to consider who will see your portfolio and what they will need or want to get from looking at the proof of your accomplishments. Your primary audience might be hiring managers, screening committees or recruiters. The secondary audience could be members of a professional association, college advisors or colleagues with whom you are networking. Another audience might be your boss during your performance review.

Audience	What They Will Want to See	Familiarity with Topic	Level of Interest/ Emotion	Questions They Might Have
Primary				
Secondary				
Other/ Possible				

The Bottom Line

Who is my audience and how will they evaluate my portfolio? Consider completeness, graphic quality and other factors.

CREATE YOUR COMMERCIAL ANNOUNCEMENT

A commercial announcement is a concise description of your skills, abilities or accomplishments that explains your talents and contributions to your audience. Someone once said we retain

25% of what we hear

45% of what we see

75% of what we see and hear.

You may question the percentages, but you can increase your memorability to others by ensuring that you reinforce as thoroughly as possible the image of yourself as a capable, productive employee.

How can you get your portfolio in front of the interviewer? During an interview, you may not control the question, but you do control the content. When someone asks, "Give me an example of a times when you . . ." or "Have you ever . . ." or "What would you do if . . . ," use a brief (30 to 60 seconds at most) statement to introduce a page or section of your portfolio.

> "I'd like to show you an example of the last project I was involved in at Xanadu. My team was asked to develop a workflow system assessment that would help managers identify and implement efficiencies. This was part of our continuous improvement process where the goal was to avoid the expense and frustration of a complete reengineering effort. My part involved developing the forms and documentation. As you can see, I needed to use my skills in forms design, layout, technical writing and interviewing. I created the forms and did the user testing, then compiled the reviews, made changes and worked with our systems group to get the templates on-line."

> "These are examples of the special management reports I designed. Frequently, managers needed to answer questions about compensation plans, or needed information about benefit costs for an operating unit. Turnaround was often very fast, so I developed my own strategy for getting the report parameters so I could respond in as little as three hours for most requests."

DESIGNING YOUR COMMERCIAL

1. Introduce yourself and your professional history

"Throughout my career, one strength has been my creativity."

2. Mention what you will show them

"I'd like to show you some examples of the training materials I've developed."

3. Introduce your examples and explain what they represent, why they are important and how they relate to the question

"This is part of a self-assessment I designed, which was included in a workbook."

4. Draw similarities between what you did elsewhere to the needs of your prospective employer

"My tasks there were much like the series that was mentioned as part of the critical element of this job."

Your Example: Take an example you plan to use and write several points about it. Talk through that commercial and make notes about what you say. Use a small tape recorder to listen to your commercial.

REMEMBER

▶ *The best commercial announcements sound as if they are spontaneous and unrehearsed*

Practice just enough to remember the key points, but don't be afraid to change your commercial. You don't want it to come out as a "recorded announcement."

▶ *Tailor the content to the audience you are addressing*

Your audience may need to know some things about you in more detail than others. Think about who you're talking to. Use brief introductory phrases: "I was involved in a major quality effort; here's an example . . ."

▶ *Become the objective observer: Are you using words that minimize the importance of your work? Is the commercial organized so that others can understand what you did and how it applies to the question they asked?*

Tape record your practice and listen for tentative words such as "maybe" or "kind of" or phrases that erase your confidence: "It wasn't much. . . ."

▶ *Be prepared to answer the follow-up questions that arise as a result of seeing your example*

Be succinct. Help the interviewer "see" you doing the job.

▶ *Your prospective employer will be so delighted to have more information on which to base a decision, he or she may want to keep your portfolio*

A graceful way of saying "no" is to offer copies of a few items or explain that you will need your portfolio for another interview, so you can't leave it.

▶ *Offer to meet with anyone they mention who would be interested in seeing your work*

Mention that you would be happy to show anyone your portfolio. This is an excellent chance to sell your experience to other decision-makers.

AN OUTLINE FOR YOUR INTERVIEW PRESENTATION

Interviews are usually fairly predictable. The employer asks questions to gain information about your background, confidence, communication skills and ability to think on your feet. Your portfolio is the evidence you bring to show what you have done. Whether you show your portfolio or not, going to an interview without preparing answers to common questions isn't likely to get you the job. Knowing what examples you want to use is also helpful when issues you would like to discuss are not raised. Saying "For example," can bridge your reply to a specific question to an example you want to introduce. *This doesn't mean you memorize answers.* It means you have some idea of what you will use for an example.

Use the following common interview questions and turn them into 250–350 words (about 90 seconds when spoken). Practice them for each of the examples in your portfolio.

SAMPLE A ——— *My comments*	**SAMPLE B** ——— *Other issues I could raise*

EXERCISE: Answering Questions

"What are your strengths?"

Example: *I've been told that I'm very creative. For example, I found that the forms that were used to collect data about our clients had a lot of space for information that wasn't needed. So I redesigned the form and presented it to my supervisor who thought it was a great idea. It took less time for clients to complete. Here's an example of the old form and the one I created.*

Your Example:

"Tell me about a project where you needed to work as part of a team."

Example: *I was part of a project team to develop a system for tracking inventory to ensure we had all advertised items in stock for a sale. Here's a sample of the report we developed to evaluate sales projections. I designed the form, tested it and wrote the directions; working with 2 other team members who also tested it.*

Your Example:

EXERCISE (continued)

"What have you been told you do best?"

Example: *My supervisor says that my ability to remember customers and their preferences contributes a lot to our department's image. This is something I learned to do when I was in my first job. People are easier to work with if they realize you care enough to remember them and what pleases them. This is a photo of our work area—as you can see, I was "front and center" all the time.*

Your Example:

"What accomplishments are you proud of?"

Example: *I'm very proud of my soccer team. We made it all the way to the state conference last year. Here's a photo of the team in a scrimmage.*

Your Example:

WHEN TO USE YOUR PORTFOLIO

Check this list against the one you brainstormed on page 10.

✓ Performance evaluations

✓ Interviews with educational counselors when returning to school

✓ Interviews with career consultants to focus on transferable skills and experience

✓ Presentations to head hunters

✓ On-line postings or your own Internet home page

✓ Displays at job fairs

✓ Job interviews

✓ Career development interviews with mentors, managers or human resources

✓ Networking sessions at professional organizations

Portfolio Log

Any item you add to your draft portfolio should be cataloged for future reference so that you don't forget why you decided to include it. Use Post-it™ tape or Zip-Loc™ baggies that can be labeled. Be conscious of confidential information or copyrights that must be considered when deciding what to include.

Item			
Date			
What I did			
Team/Coproducers			
What I learned			
Challenge in doing this			
Why it's included			
Other information			

(Make several copies of this page and use it while you assemble your portfolio to keep track of items and ideas. You can also reproduce it on your computer so that it expands along with your examples and ideas.)

FINAL PORTFOLIO CHECKLIST

Content

☐ Does your portfolio have the best examples of your accomplishments?

☐ Have you limited it to two to three examples in any category?

☐ Are the examples brief? Have you edited for clarity?

☐ Is every item in your portfolio public information? If not, have you permission to use it?

☐ Are your skills clearly demonstrated?

☐ Have you checked the spelling and grammar of everything you wrote?

Organization

☐ Is the sequence of the examples logical?

☐ Are similar items and accomplishments grouped to eliminate unnecessary page turning?

☐ Has the sequence been tested and edited?

☐ Have you used tabs and color coding to ensure you can find each item easily?

☐ Have you practiced telling a "skill story" about each sample?

FINAL PORTFOLIO CHECKLIST (continued)

Graphic Elements

☐ Have you used consistent borders and graphic styles?

☐ Are there brief labels, highlights or arrows pointing out key phrases or focal points?

☐ Does the book project a professional, organized image?

Security

☐ Do you have extra copies of your resume, work samples and references to leave behind?

☐ Have you created back-up diskettes of anything you will leave behind?

☐ Are all the pages inside sheet protectors or laminated to protect them?

CONCLUSION

By now you've discovered what a boost it can give your ego to have all your accomplishments in a single showcase. You may have learned new skills: graphic layout, editing and headline composition. When you composed your personal commercial, you prepared a sales presentation, which may also be a first for you.

Remember to keep your portfolio up-to-date. A skills portfolio isn't a static product . . . since you are learning and growing all the time, so should your portfolio. In the words of Dizzy Dean, baseball great, "It ain't braggin' if you can do it!" There may be some luck involved, but skill counts when you want to move forward in your career. Add new skills and accomplishments as they happen.

What will tomorrow hold? Your portfolio is a record of the past; it can also be a good predictor of the future, helping to define the talents and abilities that you prefer to emphasize when you job search. You'll have a competitive edge in tomorrow's fast-changing job market. Make yours the very best!

BIBLIOGRAPHY

Berrymann, Gregg. *Designing Creative Portfolios.* Menlo Park, CA: Crisp, 1994.

Hanks, Kurt and Larry Belliston. *Draw! A Visual Approach to Thinking, Learning and Communicating.* Menlo Park, CA: William Kaufmann, 1992.

Mahoney, Marci. *Strategic Resumes.* Menlo Park, CA: Crisp, 1992.

Mandel, Steve. *Effective Presentation Skills—Revised.* Menlo Park, CA: Crisp, 1993.

Wescott, Jean and Jennifer Landau. *A Picture's Worth a Thousand Words.* Self-Published, 1993.

Now Available From

⌖RISP.
Learning™

Books•Videos•CD-ROMs•Computer-Based Training Products

If you enjoyed this book, we have great news for you.
There are over 200 books available in the *Fifty-Minute™ Series*.
To request a free full-line catalog, contact your local distributor or
Crisp Learning
1200 Hamilton Court
Menlo Park, CA 94025
1-800-442-7477
CrispLearning.com

Subject Areas Include:

Management
Human Resources
Communication Skills
Personal Development
Marketing/Sales
Organizational Development
Customer Service/Quality
Computer Skills
Small Business and Entrepreneurship
Adult Literacy and Learning
Life Planning and Retirement

CRISP WORLDWIDE DISTRIBUTION

English language books are distributed worldwide. Major international distributors include:

ASIA/PACIFIC

Australia/New Zealand: In Learning, PO Box 1051, Springwood QLD, Brisbane, Australia 4127   Tel: 61-7-3-841-2286, Facsimile: 61-7-3-841-1580
ATTN: Messrs. Richard/Robert Gordon

Malaysia, Philippines, Singapore: Epsys Pte Ltd., 540 Sims Ave #04-01, Sims Avenue Centre, 387603, Singapore   Tel: 65-747-1964, Facsimile: 65-747-0162 ATTN: Mr. Jack Chin

Hong Kong/Mainland China: Crisp Learning Solutions, 18/F Honest Motors Building 9-11 Leighton Rd., Causeway Bay, Hong Kong   Tel: 852-2915-7119, Facsimile: 852-2865-2815 ATTN: Ms. Grace Lee

Japan: Phoenix Associates, Believe Mita Bldg., 8th Floor 3-43-16 Shiba, Minato-ku, Tokyo 105-0014, Japan   Tel: 81-3-5427-6231, Facsimile: 81-3-5427-6232
ATTN: Mr. Peter Owans

CANADA

Crisp Learning Canada, 60 Briarwood Avenue, Mississauga, ON L5G 3N6 Canada
Tel: 905-274-5678, Facsimile: 905-278-2801
ATTN: Mr. Steve Connolly

EUROPEAN UNION

England: Flex Learning Media, Ltd., 9-15 Hitchin Street,
Baldock, Hertfordshire, SG7 6AL, England
Tel: 44-1-46-289-6000, Facsimile: 44-1-46-289-2417   ATTN: Mr. David Willetts

INDIA

Multi-Media HRD, Pvt. Ltd., National House, Floor 1
6 Tulloch Road, Appolo Bunder, Bombay, India 400-039
Tel: 91-22-204-2281, Facsimile: 91-22-283-6478
ATTN: Messrs. Ajay Aggarwal/ C.L. Aggarwal

SOUTH AMERICA

Mexico: Grupo Editorial Iberoamerica, Nebraska 199, Col. Napoles, 03810 Mexico, D.F.
Tel: 525-523-0994, Facsimile: 525-543-1173   ATTN: Señor Nicholas Grepe

SOUTH AFRICA

Bookstores: Alternative Books, PO Box 1345, Ferndale 2160, South Africa
Tel: 27-11-792-7730, Facsimile: 27-11-792-7787   ATTN: Mr. Vernon de Haas

Corporate: Learning Resources, P.O. Box 2806, Parklands, Johannesburg 2121, South Africa, Tel: 27-21-531-2923, Facsimile: 27-21-531-2944 ATTN: Mr. Ricky Robinson

MIDDLE EAST

Edutech Middle East, L.L.C., PO Box 52334, Dubai U.A.E.
Tel: 971-4-359-1222, Facsimile: 971-4-359-6500   ATTN: Mr. A.S.F. Karim